41352

READING POWER

Coming to America

Why German Immigrants Came to America

Lewis K. Parker

The Rosen Publishing Group's
PowerKids Press™
New York

Published in 2003 by The Rosen Publishing Group, Inc.
29 East 21st Street, New York, NY 10010

First Edition

Book Design: Erica Clendening and Mindy Liu

Photo Credits: Cover, p. 14 (inset) © AP/WideWorld; pp. 4–5, 15 (maps) Erica Clendening; pp. 5, 8–9 © North Wind Picture Archives; pp. 7, 12–13, 19 © Hulton/Archive/Gettty Images; pp. 14–15 courtesy of the Denver Public Library, Western History Collection, X-2275; pp. 17 (top and bottom), 18, 21 (bottom) Library of Congress, Prints and Photographs Division; p. 20 © Nigel Marple/REUTERS/ Timepix; p. 21 (top) © Dave Allocca/DMI/Timepix

Library of Congress Cataloging-in-Publication Data

Parker, Lewis K.
Why German immigrants came to America / Lewis K. Parker.
    p. cm. — (Coming to America)
Summary: Explores German immigration to the United States from colonial days to the present, and looks at the contributions of German Americans to the culture of the United States.
Includes bibliographical references and index.
ISBN 0-8239-6458-2 (alk. paper)
1. German Americans—History—Juvenile literature. 2.
Immigrants—United States—History—Juvenile literature. 3. United States—Emigration and immigration—History—Juvenile literature. 4. Germany—Emigration and immigration—History—Juvenile literature. [1. German Americans—History. 2. Immigrants—History. 3. Germany—Emigration and immigration. 4. United States—Emigration and immigration.] I. Title.
E184.G3 P37 2003
304.8'73043—dc21

                                             2002000111

Contents

Early Settlement

One of the first groups of German immigrants came to America in 1683. Thirteen families came to the American colonies so that they could follow their religion freely. The immigrants settled near Philadelphia, Pennsylvania. They called their settlement Germantown.

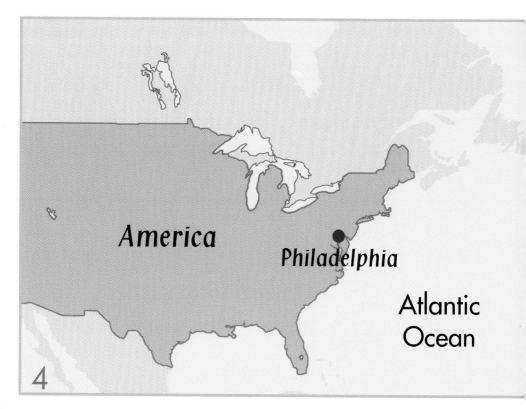

America

Philadelphia

Atlantic Ocean

Many early German immigrants made their living as farmers.

Germany

Immigrants from Germany sailed halfway around the world seeking religious freedom.

A Better Way of Life

More German immigrants came to America in the 1700s. Foreign armies were attacking Germany. Many people in Germany wanted to start a new life in a safe place. By 1775, about 225,000 Germans had immigrated to America.

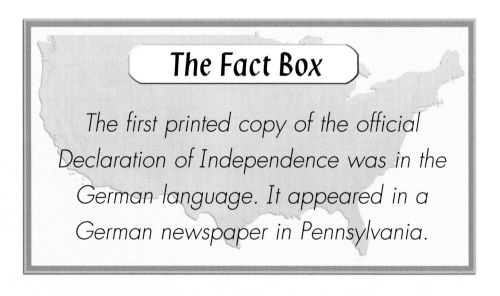

The Fact Box

The first printed copy of the official Declaration of Independence was in the German language. It appeared in a German newspaper in Pennsylvania.

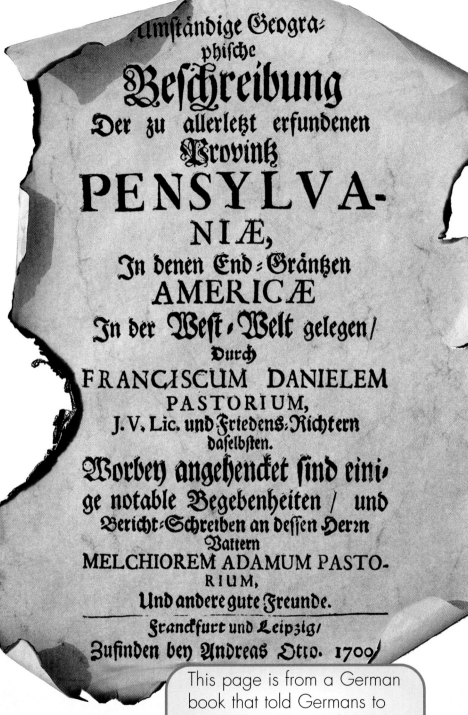

Umständige Geogra-
phische
Beschreibung
Der zu allerletzt erfundenen
Provintz
PENSYLVA-
NIÆ,
In denen End-Gräntzen
AMERICÆ
In der **West-Welt** gelegen /
Durch
FRANCISCUM DANIELEM
PASTORIUM,
J. V. Lic. und Friedens-Richtern
daselbsten.
**Worbey angehencket sind eini-
ge notable Begebenheiten / und**
Bericht-Schreiben an dessen Herrn
Vattern
MELCHIOREM ADAMUM PASTO-
RIUM,
Und andere gute Freunde.

Franckfurt und Leipzig/
Zufinden bey Andreas Otto. 1700/

This page is from a German book that told Germans to immigrate to Pennsylvania.

When harvests were good, German farmers sold their crops at the marketplace. When their crops failed, many farmers came to America.

During the 1800s, many factories in Germany started to use machines to make products. Many people who were making the same products by hand lost their jobs. Farmers had poor harvests, too. Many German immigrants came to America to find jobs and a better way of life.

Traveling to America

In the early years of German immigration, people came to America on sailing ships. The trip took months. Living conditions on the ships were very bad. Many passengers became sick and died.

German immigrants often stayed below deck on their boat trip. Some of them did not get a breath of fresh air until the end of their trip.

By 1870, German immigrants traveled on steamships. Steamships could cross the Atlantic Ocean in about two to three weeks. Living conditions on steamships were safer than on the sailing ships.

Many Germans took steamships to New York City and Philadelphia.

Most German immigrants arrived in cities on the east coast of America. Then they moved to cities and towns near their families and friends who had already settled in America.

German Immigration During the 1800s	
Year	Number
1820–29	5,753
1830–39	124,726
1840–49	385,434
1850–59	976,072
1860–69	723,734
1870–79	751,769
1880–89	1,445,181
1890–99	579,072

Some German immigrants traveled west across rivers, plains, and mountains. They built new towns in the Midwest and West. They were pioneers.

Levi Strauss made the first pair of blue jeans in 1850. In 1853, he went to San Francisco to sell blue jeans to miners.

Some Germans opened places to stay for travelers going west.

Large German Populations in the United States

Milwaukee, WI

Germantown, PA

St. Louis, MO

Cincinnati, OH

Anaheim, CA

GERMAN HOUSE

15

German Americans at Work

Many German immigrants worked as farmers in their new home. German immigrants also worked as bakers, butchers, blacksmiths, shoemakers, cigar makers, maids, nurses, and tailors.

The Fact Box

In 1856, a German immigrant started the first kindergarten in Watertown, Wisconsin.

Many women who immigrated to America worked as nurses.

German American blacksmiths made tools.

17

Another large group of German immigrants came in the 1930s and 1940s. These immigrants were escaping Adolf Hitler's Nazi government. Many scientists, writers, and musicians came to America during this time.

Thomas Mann was a German writer who immigrated to America.

Albert Einstein, a German immigrant, was one of the most important scientists in history.

German Immigrants Today

Since 1950, more than one million Germans have immigrated to America. In 1990, over 58 million Americans said they had a German background. German immigrants have played an important part in the growth of America.

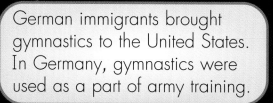

German immigrants brought gymnastics to the United States. In Germany, gymnastics were used as a part of army training.

The Fact Box

Many popular foods were introduced to America by German immigrants. Hamburgers, frankfurters, and candy corn are some of these foods.

The plans for the Brooklyn Bridge in New York City were made by John Augustus Roebling, a German immigrant.

Glossary

blacksmiths (**blak**-smiths) people who make objects out of iron by heating and hammering the iron

determination (dih-tehr-muh-**nay**-shuhn) firmness in doing what you have planned

foreign (**for**-uhn) coming from outside your own country

gymnastics (jihm-**nas**-tihks) difficult exercises involving carefully controlled movements

harvests (**hahr**-vihsts) the crops picked at the end of a growing season

immigrants (**ihm**-uh-gruhnts) people who come into a country to live there

pioneers (py-uh-**nihrz**) people who go first and get the way ready for others

settlement (**seht**-l-mehnt) a place where people come to live

Resources

Books

German Americans, 1820—1920
by Helen Frost
Capstone Press (2001)

The German Americans
by Anne Galicich
Chelsea House Publishers (1996)

Web Sites

Due to the changing nature of Internet links, PowerKids Press has developed an online list of Web sites related to the subject of this book. This site is updated regularly. Please use this link to access the list:

http://www.powerkidslinks.com/cta/ger/

Index

B
blacksmiths, 16–17

C
colonies, 4

F
factories, 9

G
Germantown, 4, 15

H
harvests, 8–9

M
Midwest, 14

P
Philadelphia, 4, 12
pioneers, 14

S
sailing ships, 10, 12
settlement, 4
steamships, 12

W
West, 14

Word Count: 383

Note to Librarians, Teachers, and Parents

If reading is a challenge, Reading Power is a solution! Reading Power is perfect for readers who want high-interest subject matter at an accessible reading level. These fact-filled, photo-illustrated books are designed for readers who want straightforward vocabulary, engaging topics, and a manageable reading experience. With clear picture/text correspondence, leveled Reading Power books put the reader in charge. Now readers have the power to get the information they want and the skills they need in a user-friendly format.